VELOCITY

AMERICAN SPECIAL OPS

THE U.S. ARMY RANGERS
The Missions

by William Caper

Consultant:
Travis James West
Midwest Regional Director
U.S. Army Ranger Association

CAPSTONE PRESS
a capstone imprint

Velocity is published by Capstone Press,
1710 Roe Crest Drive, North Mankato, Minnesota 56003.
www.capstonepub.com

Library of Congress Cataloging-in-Publication Data
Caper, William.
The U.S. Army Rangers : the missions / by William Caper.
p. cm.—(Velocity. American special ops)
Includes bibliographical references and index.
Audience: Ages 10-12.
Summary: "Describes the U.S. Army Rangers, including the group's history,
    weapons, gear, and missions"—Provided by publisher.
ISBN 978-1-4296-8659-4 (library binding)
ISBN 978-1-62065-355-5 (ebook pdf)
1. United States. Army—Commando troops—Juvenile literature. I. Title.
UA34.R36C37 2013
356'.1670973—dc23   2012006790

Editorial Credits
Jennifer Besel, editor; Veronica Correia, designer; Laura Manthe,
    production specialist

Photo Credits
Corbis: Master Sgt. Ken Hammond, 43; Getty Images: Andrew Lichtenstein, 24 (bottom), Liaison/
Scott Peterson, 38, Time Life Pictures/Thomas D. Mcavoy, 42–43; Newscom: EPA/Erik S. Lesser,
15 (top), KRT/HO, 39, MAXPPP/Christopher Petit Tesson, 27; Shutterstock: Brent Wong, 32 (.50
caliber), Digital Storm, 5 (silhouette), Johan Swanepoel, 5 (globe), Michal Baranski, 9, Vartanov
Anatoly, 32 (M9 and M4A1); U.S. Air Force photo, 12–13, Airman 1st Class George Goslin,
20–21, Senior Airman Alexandra Hoachlander, 34 (M203), Senior Airman Jason Epley, 19, 40,
Staff Sgt. Jonathan Cole, 32 (M82A1), Staff Sgt. Luke P. Thelen, 8, Tech Sgt. Francisco V. Govea
II, 37 (Stryker); U.S. Army photo, 16–17, 37 (motorcycle), Capt. Manuel Menedez, 75th Army
Rangers, 15 (bottom), Edward N. Johnson, 28 (top), 44 (right), 45 (right), cover, Gary L. Kieffer,
5, Jessica Bruckert, USASOC PAO, 14, John D. Helms, 24 (top), Master Sgt. Cecilio Ricardo, 18, 22,
23, 25, Michael Lemke, 36, Nancy Fischer, USASOC, 34 (M3), 44–45, Pfc. Cameron Boyd, 40–41,
Sgt. Marcus Butler, USASOC Public Affairs, 10, Sgt. Zachary Gardner, 20, Spc. Jennifer J. Eidsen,
USASOC PAO, 45 (left), Spc. Joshua E. Powell, 28 (bottom), Spc. Michael J. Macleod, 29, Staff Sgt.
Mark Burrell, 26 (top), US Army Africa, 4, 44 (left), USASOC Public Affairs, 11 (both), 41; U.S.
Navy photo by MC2 (DSW/SW) Christopher Perez, 8-9, MC2 Matthew D. Leistikow, 26 (bottom);
Wikimedia: OpenStreetMap, 12, U.S Army, 17, 32 (MK48), U.S. Army, USASOC, 32 (MK46), U.S.
Army photo by Sergeant James McCauley, 30

Artist Effects
Shutterstock

Printed in the United States of America in Stevens Point, Wisconsin.

TABLE OF CONTENTS

ON THE MOVE

Under the cover of night, three helicopters slice through the air. They land near a building, and 24 U.S. Army Rangers leap out. Moving quickly, the Rangers race to the building and drop to the ground. Their clothes blend in with their surroundings. Wearing night-vision goggles, a Ranger fires a grenade at the door. The grenade explodes and blasts through the door. Before the smoke clears, the Rangers pour into the building, ready to fire.

Enemy soldiers are inside, and the Rangers have caught them by surprise. Moving through the building in small teams, the Rangers defeat the enemy soldiers. They also find computer files that reveal the enemy's future plans.

Who are these skilled soldiers? They are members of the largest special operations combat unit in the U.S. Army, the 75th Ranger Regiment. The Ranger Regiment specializes in missions deep inside enemy territory. The regiment is made up of four battalions.

THE RANGER BATTALIONS HAVE THREE DIFFERENT HOME BASES.

2nd Ranger Battalion
Fort Lewis, Washington

1st Ranger Battalion
Hunter Army Airfield, Georgia

3rd Ranger Battalion and the Special Troops Battalion
Fort Benning, Georgia

Ranger battalions take turns being on "ready" status. This status means the battalion can be sent on a mission at any time. When on "ready" status, a battalion can deploy anywhere in the world with just 18 hours notice.

Chapter 1

WHO RANGERS ARE

U.S. Army Rangers have a long history going back to before the United States was founded. They have always been a different kind of soldier. Rangers never stood in lines, firing weapons at the same time. Instead they hid behind trees and rocks and fired when they had a clear shot at the enemy. With this fighting style, small groups of Rangers often won battles against much larger forces.

Captain Benjamin Church formed one of the first American Ranger units during King Philip's War. This war was between American Indians and English colonists. Rangers were successful because they used tactics learned from the Indians.

During the Revolutionary War, colonists formed groups of expert riflemen to fight British soldiers. They were often called the Corps of Rangers.

Major Robert Rogers led Rangers during the French and Indian War. These Rangers fought in small groups. Instead of wearing uniforms, they wore clothes that blended in with nature.

1754-1763

During the War of 1812, Rangers patrolled the frontier from Ohio to western Illinois. They fought British troops and their American Indian allies.

Fact

Before he was U.S. president, Abraham Lincoln belonged to a Ranger unit.

1861-1865

During the American Civil War, both the North and South used Ranger units. Fighting on horseback, Rangers moved swiftly from place to place, raiding enemy camps and supply bases.

1950-1953

During the Korean War, small Ranger companies fought where regular troops needed the help of special operations units. Rangers scouted, patrolled, and conducted raids.

During World War II, Rangers took part in many operations. As part of the D-Day Allied invasion of Europe, Rangers climbed 100-foot (30-meter) cliffs. They captured key German positions that threatened Allied troops.

1939-1945

During the Vietnam War, the Army again created Ranger units. The Rangers conducted special operations behind enemy lines. These missions included scouting, gathering information, and rescuing prisoners of war.

1959-1975

colonist—a person who settles in a new territory governed by his or her home country

ally—a person or country united with another for a common purpose

raid—a sudden, surprise attack on a place

MODERN RANGERS

After each war in which Rangers fought, the Ranger units were broken up. However, one year before the end of the Vietnam War, U.S. military leaders decided to form a permanent group of these highly-trained soldiers. The first permanent Ranger battalion was formed in 1974. Since then, Rangers have conducted operations all over the world.

Why send Rangers? Sometimes sending a large army into combat is not a good idea. Rangers are specially trained to fight in small groups. They have high-tech gear that helps them fight at night. They **ambush** the enemy and avoid attacks themselves. They are trained to work in difficult environments, such as swamps and mountains.

ambush—a surprise attack

Missions around the World

OPERATION JUST CAUSE IN PANAMA

Rangers seized Torrijos-Tocumen Airport and Rio Hato Airport.
See page 42 for more information.

OPERATION URGENT FURY IN GRENADA

Rangers seized Point Salines Airport and rescued American medical students.
See page 12 for more information.

OPERATION ANACONDA IN AFGHANISTAN

Rangers conducted missions against al-Qaida and the Taliban.
See page 16 for more information.

Afghanistan

Iraq

Grenada

Somalia

Panama

OPERATION GOTHIC SERPENT IN SOMALIA

Rangers fought in the Battle of Mogadishu.
See page 39 for more information.

OPERATION IRAQI FREEDOM IN IRAQ

Rangers conducted missions in support of U.S. troops and their allies.
See page 30 for more information.

TYPES OF MISSIONS

Rangers will do whatever U.S. military leaders ask of them. They are trained to do many kinds of missions.

Direct Action

Direct action missions are carried out to fight enemy soldiers directly. To do this, Rangers surprise and quickly overwhelm the enemy. They might fly in on helicopters and slide down ropes to the ground or a rooftop. In Operation Urgent Fury and Operation Just Cause, Rangers arrived in airplanes and parachuted to the ground. Once on the ground, they fought enemies using rifles, machine guns, and grenade launchers.

Sensitive Site Exploitation

Rangers don't leave immediately when a site is taken over. When Rangers capture a site, they look for information about enemies and their plans. This information might be used to plan future missions.

Airfield Seizure

Some missions require Rangers to seize an airfield in enemy territory. During Operation Just Cause, Rangers seized two airfields. The Rangers' successful missions stopped the enemy from using the airfields and allowed the United States to bring in supplies and more troops.

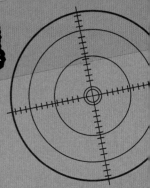

IN ACTION!

OPERATION URGENT FURY
Grenada, 1983

BACKGROUND: In 1983 Grenada's elected government was overthrown. The U.S. government became concerned about the safety of American students attending medical school there. There was a lot of violence, and it was feared that the students might be hurt.

RANGER MISSION: Take control of Point Salines Airfield and rescue the American students attending St. George's University.

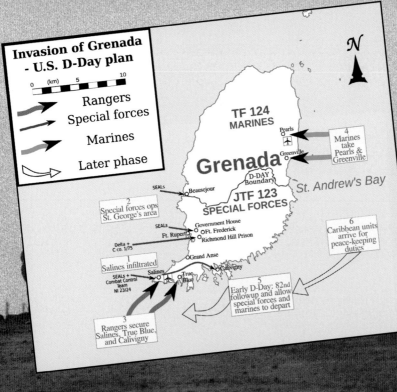

Invasion of Grenada - U.S. D-Day plan

0   (km)   5   10

→ Rangers
→ Special forces
→ Marines
⇨ Later phase

N

TF 124 MARINES

Pearls

4 Marines take Pearls & Greenville

Grenada
Greenville

D-DAY Boundary

St. Andrew's Bay

SEALs Beausejour

JTF 123 SPECIAL FORCES

2 Special forces ops St. George's area

SEALs Government House
Ft. Rupert ○ Ft. Frederick
○ Richmond Hill Prison

Delta + C Co. 1/75

○ Grand Anse

6 Caribbean units arrive for peace-keeping duties

Salines infiltrated

SEALS + Combat Control Team NI 23/24

Salines ✈ ○ True Blue

○ Calivigny

5 Early D-Day: 82nd followup and allow special forces and marines to depart

3 Rangers secure Salines, True Blue, and Calivigny

Day One: October 25

About 600 Rangers parachuted onto Point Salines Airfield. Enemy soldiers fired at them as they landed, but the Rangers kept going. After the Rangers silenced the enemy fire, two-man teams cleared away vehicles blocking the runway.

Another group of Rangers began the second part of the mission. This group arrived at the True Blue campus of St. George's University. The Rangers found about 140 students. The Rangers then learned of a larger campus with about 200 students a few miles to the north at Grand Anse. The Rangers hadn't known about this campus, and they had no plans to capture it.

Day Two: October 26

Overnight, Rangers planned a mission to capture the second campus. Flying in on six helicopters, Rangers seized the Grand Anse campus. They found 233 students and led them to the helicopters.

Day Three: October 27

While waiting to go home, the Rangers got an unexpected mission. They were to secure the Calivigny military barracks where enemy soldiers were thought to be living. Three U.S. helicopters were damaged in the attack. But the Rangers quickly completed their mission.

Day Four: October 28

With their missions accomplished, the Rangers went back to Point Salines Airfield. The next day they left Grenada.

barracks—housing for soldiers

Fact

The rescue at the Grand Anse campus took just 26 minutes to complete.

Special Reconnaissance

Special reconnaissance (SR) is dangerous, secret work. These missions require Rangers to go into enemy territory to gather information. On SR missions, Rangers gather details that would be impossible to get with a machine. Commanders use the information to plan attacks or other missions.

Rangers on SR missions sometimes help guide pilots to secret enemy locations. The pilots can then fly over and use missiles or other weapons to destroy the enemy targets.

reconnaissance—a mission to gather information about an enemy

Clandestine Insertion

The key to these missions is complete secrecy. On clandestine insertion missions, Rangers sneak into enemy territory to attack. On some missions, Rangers hide and wait to ambush the enemy. On other missions, they attack immediately.

Personnel Recovery

Personnel recovery missions send Rangers into an area to get people out. Sometimes these missions are carried out to rescue prisoners of war or civilians and soldiers who are in trouble.

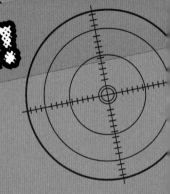

OPERATION ANACONDA
Battle of Takur Ghar
Afghanistan, 2002

BACKGROUND: After the attacks of September 11, 2001, the United States sent troops to Afghanistan to combat the Taliban and al-Qaida. In 2002 al-Qaida fighters were discovered in the Shah-i-Kot valley. Operation Anaconda was launched to remove them.

RANGER MISSION: Rescue American military members outnumbered by enemy forces.

bunker—a room or building set beneath the ground to offer protection during war

The Events:

Two Chinook helicopters carrying special ops soldiers headed to a mountain called Takur Ghar. As one helicopter was landing, it was hit by a rocket-propelled grenade (RPG) and machine gun fire. When the helicopter retreated, a Navy SEAL fell out. The pilot was able to land the damaged helicopter 4 miles (6 km) away. But the SEAL was alone on the mountain.

The second helicopter picked up the men from the damaged one. It dropped a team of six special ops soldiers on the mountain to rescue the fallen SEAL. But the team soon became overwhelmed by enemy fire and had to move down the mountain.

Back at base, two teams of Rangers boarded two other helicopters to rescue the special ops soldiers. As one of the Rangers' helicopters tried to land on the mountain, the enemies opened fire. The helicopter crashed. Rangers leaped out and attacked. But enemy fighters were firing from a bunker the Rangers couldn't destroy.

The Rangers radioed their base for air support. U.S. aircraft soon dropped bombs on the enemy bunker.

Meanwhile, the second Ranger helicopter landed more than 2,000 feet (610 m) down the mountain. From there Rangers climbed the mountain. They had to wade through deep snow under enemy fire. It took them two hours to reach the mountaintop. When they finally arrived, both groups of Rangers attacked and defeated the enemy soldiers.

Ending:

Commanders waited until after dark to send helicopters to pick up the U.S. soldiers. Al-Qaida soldiers continued to fight to recapture the mountaintop. But air strikes by U.S. aircraft stopped them.

This event is known as the Battle of Takur Ghar. Seven U.S. servicemen were killed in the battle, including the SEAL who fell from the helicopter.

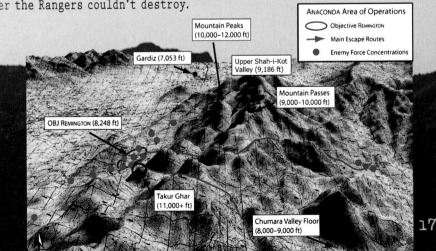

ANACONDA Area of Operations
- Objective REMINGTON
- Main Escape Routes
- Enemy Force Concentrations

Mountain Peaks (10,000–12,000 ft)

Gardiz (7,053 ft)

Upper Shah-i-Kot Valley (9,186 ft)

Mountain Passes (9,000–10,000 ft)

OBJ REMINGTON (8,248 ft)

Takur Ghar (11,000+ ft)

Chumara Valley Floor (8,000–9,000 ft)

BECOMING A RANGER

Rangers have to be strong. But they must also be smart, courageous, and disciplined. They must not give up easily. Becoming a Ranger is a long, hard process.

Step 1 – Join the Army

The first step in becoming a Ranger is joining the Army. Army recruits must say they want to be Rangers. These recruits get what is called an Option 40 contract. This contract puts potential Rangers on a slightly different training course than regular Army soldiers.

Step 2 – One Station Unit Training (OSUT)

Soldiers with a Ranger contract enter a 14-week training school. In OSUT, soldiers exercise and learn rifle marksmanship. They learn how to use and maintain vehicles. They also learn **navigation** and how to use communication equipment. Then they put all their skills to the test in battle drills.

navigation—the science of plotting and following a course from one place to another

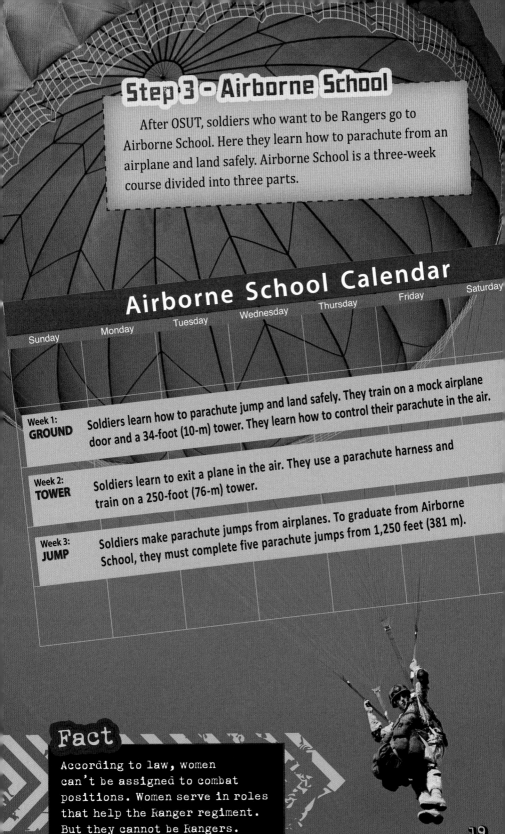

Step 3 - Airborne School

After OSUT, soldiers who want to be Rangers go to Airborne School. Here they learn how to parachute from an airplane and land safely. Airborne School is a three-week course divided into three parts.

Airborne School Calendar

Sunday	Monday	Tuesday	Wednesday	Thursday	Friday	Saturday
Week 1: GROUND	Soldiers learn how to parachute jump and land safely. They train on a mock airplane door and a 34-foot (10-m) tower. They learn how to control their parachute in the air.					
Week 2: TOWER	Soldiers learn to exit a plane in the air. They use a parachute harness and train on a 250-foot (76-m) tower.					
Week 3: JUMP	Soldiers make parachute jumps from airplanes. To graduate from Airborne School, they must complete five parachute jumps from 1,250 feet (381 m).					

Fact

According to law, women can't be assigned to combat positions. Women serve in roles that help the Ranger regiment. But they cannot be Rangers.

RASP

Next soldiers must pass the Ranger Assessment and Selection Program (RASP). RASP training includes physical fitness, marksmanship, small unit **tactics**, and first aid.

Cole Range

In the second week of RASP, the men spend four days at Cole Range. During this time, they sleep only about four hours a day. They train in patrolling and land navigation. At any time of the day or night, they might be ordered to carry out an exercise. During winter training sometimes more than 40 percent of the men quit during the first night.

Ranger Swim Ability Evaluation

For the swim test, a student enters a swimming pool wearing body armor. He must go underwater, remove his armor, and return to the surface. Then he must swim 328 feet (100 m) without showing signs of fear or panic.

tactic—an action taken to achieve a goal

RASP is so difficult that sometimes less than one-third of the men who enter graduate. The following are just a few samples of the tasks soldiers must complete.

Ranger First Responder (RFR)

This course teaches first aid and lifesaving procedures for combat. Soldiers learn to clear airways, control bleeding, and care for serious wounds.

Soldiers can quit at any time. They can also be dropped from the program if they don't pass the tests. These soldiers do not join the 75th Ranger Regiment. They are sent to other army units.

Soldiers who successfully complete RASP are assigned to a battalion in the 75th Regiment. They are now officially Rangers. However, their training is far from over. In order to rise in rank and lead other men in the 75th Regiment, they have to go to Ranger School.

RANGER SCHOOL

Ranger School is one of the most difficult military programs in the world. Only about half of the men who start the program graduate. There are three phases to Ranger School.

Benning Phase

Phase 1 of Ranger School is held at Fort Benning, Georgia. The Rangers' physical fitness and land combat skills are improved and tested.

Students must prove they are fearless in the water during the Combat Water Survival Assessment. One test has Rangers climb to the top of a 75-foot (23-m) tower. From the top, students slide down on a pulley attached to a cable and drop into the water.

During the land navigation test, students must find locations in the dark without flashlights. The locations are identified by numbers. Students must find them using only a map and a compass.

Students must complete several obstacle courses during Benning Phase. The Darby Queen course is about 1 mile (1.6 km) long and has more than 20 obstacles.

Mountain Phase

The second phase of Ranger School lasts 21 days and takes place at Camp Frank D. Merrill in Georgia. There, students receive mountaineering training.

3 The soldiers' leadership skills are also tested. At any time, a student can be chosen to lead other students on a new mission.

2 During mountain phase, students go on day and night Field Training Exercises (FTX). These exercises train students to move across mountains. FTX also give students practice in ambushes, raids, and scaling steep mountains.

1 During the beginning of this phase, students learn:
- how to tie climbing knots.
- how to maintain their ropes so they are safe to use.
- how to climb and descend by rope.

Florida Phase

The third phase of Ranger School lasts 20 days and is conducted at Camp James E. Rudder in Florida.

Students receive training in moving through swamps and jungles. They also learn how to operate small boats and cross streams and rivers.

Rangers must live off the land during the third phase of Ranger School.

Students learn about reptiles during this phase too. Instructors teach them how to stay safe from alligators. Students also learn how to tell which snakes are poisonous. They even learn how to kill, cook, and eat snakes for survival.

Students engage in FTX that include action against a fictional enemy. They conduct raids and ambushes against this enemy. Students must practice the kinds of operations Rangers conduct for real.

Ranger Tab

Rangers who pass Ranger School earn the Ranger tab. It is an honor to wear the black and gold symbol. When a soldier from the 75th Ranger Regiment goes to Ranger School, he is often told to come back "with a tab or on a slab." In other words, he must graduate and earn the Ranger tab or die trying.

RANGER

Chapter 3

WEAPONS AND GEAR

Rangers are highly trained and skilled soldiers. But they do need tools to help them complete their missions. They also need gear to help keep them safe.

GPS LOCATOR

A Global Positioning System (GPS) locator pinpoints a location. The GPS communicates with satellites in space around Earth. Rangers use this device to measure how far they are from a particular location.

NIGHT-VISION EQUIPMENT

Night-vision equipment allows Rangers to see at night or in low light. Some night-vision equipment collects small amounts of light the eyes can't see. Then it increases it so an image is visible. Other night-vision equipment works by detecting heat from objects. Hotter objects, such as bodies, give off more heat than cooler objects, such as trees or buildings.

HELMET

A lightweight helmet allows for easy movement. It also provides protection from bullets and grenade fragments. Ranger helmets are designed to be easy to use with communication headsets and microphones.

BODY ARMOR

This vest has ceramic plates inside. The plates protect the body from bullets and grenade fragments.

GLOVES

Gloves protect Rangers' hands when they fast-rope to the ground from helicopters. Some gloves also provide protection from the cold.

KNEEPADS

Kneepads protect Rangers' knees from getting hurt if slammed on hard surfaces.

COMBAT BOOTS

Boots keep soldiers' feet dry and warm. Boots may be cold-weather boots or hot-weather boots, depending on the mission. Cold-weather boots have insulation for protection from the cold.

Communication Gear

Anything can happen in combat. For a mission to go well, Rangers have to be able to communicate with one another.

RADIOS

The Ranger Communication System consists of a microphone and headset. Rangers can use radios to communicate with their commanders at their base. They can also ask for aircraft to carry out strikes.

COMPUTERS

Rangers use computers to communicate with one another. Their keyboards are sealed to keep out dust and liquid. Their screens resist scratches. And their cases won't easily break if the computer is dropped on a hard surface.

SATELLITES

The U.S. military has many satellites in orbit around Earth. These satellites can focus on a small area, gather information, and send it to the Rangers' computers.

Unmanned Aerial Vehicles

Unmanned Aerial Vehicles (UAVs) are aircraft that do not have human pilots. Rangers and other special ops forces use UAVs for missions that are extremely dangerous.

UAVs are used for two main types of missions. Equipped with cameras, they perform reconnaissance missions. Armed with missiles, they carry out attacks.

Some UAVs are operated like remote-controlled cars. They are guided by people who may be thousands of miles away. Others fly on their own, guided by computer.

Rangers hand-launch the Raven UAV.

Depending on size, UAVs range in weight from less than 1 pound (454 grams) to more than 40,000 pounds (18,144 kg).

Fact

Radio messages are sometimes spoken in code so the enemy can't understand them.

IN ACTION!

OPERATION IRAQI FREEDOM
Iraq, 2003

BACKGROUND: Haditha Dam is located on the Euphrates River in Iraq. During the war in Iraq, American commanders were concerned that enemy forces would destroy the dam and flood southern Iraq.

RANGER MISSION: Seize Haditha Dam and prevent it from being destroyed.

Haditha Dam

MARCH 31

Rangers head out to the dam. When they arrive, they find no Iraqi forces. The Rangers drive up the hill on which the dam stands. There are 12 large buildings.

After only a few buildings are secured, Iraqi soldiers open fire from the bottom of the hill. The Rangers return fire, and the enemy soldiers retreat a short distance. However, Iraqi troops continue to attack in waves. There is at least one attack every 30 minutes.

APRIL 1

Iraqi forces continue attempts to take the dam. The Rangers return fire and keep the Iraqi troops from retaking the dam.

APRIL 2

At dawn, the Rangers are attacked by artillery fire. They radio for aircraft to drop bombs on the artillery positions. Eventually the Iraqi forces leave, but the Rangers expect more attacks.

APRIL 4

The enemy troops move to a new position. They again fire artillery at the Rangers. Rangers radio for aircraft, and U.S. air strikes soon silence one of the Iraqi artillery guns. However, enemy artillery fire continues all day. The Rangers return fire, but they cannot stop the enemy guns. By the end of the day, the enemy has fired more than 350 artillery shells at the dam.

APRIL 5

Enemy artillery fire finally stops. The Rangers secure more buildings. They find a stash of Iraqi weapons and ammunition.

APRIL 6

Enemy artillery fire begins again, but there are only a few shells. Finally, word comes that the Rangers holding the dam will be relieved. They hold the dam and buildings for two more days until other units take their place.

artillery—large guns, such as cannons or missile launchers, that require several soldiers to load, aim, and fire

Weapons

Rangers engage the enemy in different ways. Sometimes they fight from a distance and sometimes they fight in close combat. Their weapons are chosen based on a mission's needs and what each weapon can do.

	RATE OF FIRE
M4A1 CARBINE RIFLE	SINGLE SHOT (MOST OFTEN) THIS RIFLE HAS AN AUTOMATIC OPTION THAT FIRES 700–950 ROUNDS PER MINUTE.
.50 CALIBER HEAVY MACHINE GUN	450–550 ROUNDS PER MINUTE
BARRETT M82A1 LONG RANGE SNIPER RIFLE	SINGLE SHOT
M9 BERETTA PISTOL	SINGLE SHOT
MK46 LIGHTWEIGHT MACHINE GUN	725 ROUNDS PER MINUTE
MK48 LIGHTWEIGHT MACHINE GUN	680–780 ROUNDS PER MINUTE

WEIGHT	EFFECTIVE RANGE	SPECIAL FEATURES/BEST MISSION USES
6.6 POUNDS (3 KG) LOADED WITH MAGAZINE	1,969 FEET (600 M)	CAN BE FITTED WITH NIGHT-VISION DEVICES, LASER POINTERS, TELESCOPIC SIGHTS, AND GRENADE LAUNCHERS
83.8 POUNDS (38 KG) 127.8 POUNDS (58 KG) WITH TRIPOD	4,921 FEET (1,500 M) FOR A POINT TARGET	THIS WEAPON IS OFTEN MOUNTED ON VEHICLES. IT IS USED FOR FIGHTING FROM A DISTANCE.
32.5 POUNDS (15 KG)	3,281 FEET (1,000 M) FOR A POINT TARGET A RANGER MADE A SHOT FROM 7,546 FEET (2,300 M) WITH IT DURING OPERATION IRAQI FREEDOM.	SNIPERS CAREFULLY HIDE AND SHOOT AT ONE ENEMY SOLDIER AT A TIME.
2.1 POUNDS (1 KG) UNLOADED	164 FEET (50 M)	A REVERSIBLE MAGAZINE RELEASE BUTTON CAN BE POSITIONED FOR EITHER RIGHT- OR LEFT-HANDED SHOOTERS. THIS WEAPON IS USED FOR CLOSE COMBAT.
15 POUNDS (6.8 KG) WHEN EMPTY; 22 POUNDS (10 KG) LOADED WITH 200 ROUNDS	2,625 FEET (800 M) FOR A POINT TARGET	THE MK46 HAS A TWO-LEGGED STAND CALLED A BIPOD FOR USE IN GROUND OPERATIONS. THIS WEAPON IS USED FOR BOTH CLOSE COMBAT AND FIGHTING FROM A DISTANCE.
18.6 POUNDS (8.4 KG)	2,625 FEET (800 M) FOR A POINT TARGET 11,811 FEET (3,600 M) FOR AN AREA TARGET	THE MK48 AND MK46 SHOOT DIFFERENT TYPES OF AMMUNITION. HOWEVER, THEY HAVE MANY PARTS IN COMMON. RANGERS USING THESE WEAPONS IN COMBAT CAN LEND EACH OTHER PARTS IF A REPAIR IS NEEDED.

M203 40 mm Grenade Launcher

- attaches to the underside of the M4 rifle
- fires high-explosive and special-purpose grenades
- can fire grenades about 1,300 feet (400 m)
- does not interrupt normal use of the weapon it is attached to

M3 Carl Gustav

- This antitank weapon is often called the Ranger Anti-Armor Weapon System (RAAWS).
- It is often used against vehicles, but has other uses depending on the type of shell fired.

The RAAWS is sometimes used as a "bunker buster." A bunker buster is a weapon or bomb designed to destroy bunkers or targets buried deep underground. When the RAAWS is used as a bunker buster, it fires a high-explosive shell. These shells produce very powerful explosions. They can destroy targets that can't be damaged by ordinary bombs.

Javelin Antitank Weapon System

The Javelin is another very powerful weapon. It shoots a **warhead** that can tear through any known armor.

Rangers use the Command Launch Unit (CLU) on the Javelin to find targets. They also use the CLU to tell the weapon's missile where to go.

To fire the Javelin, a gunner finds the target in the CLU. He then places a cursor box over the target and sends a command to the missile. The missile automatically guides itself to the target.

Rangers, Lead the Way!

On June 6, 1944, Rangers took part in the D-Day invasion of Normandy during World War II. Heavy German machine gun fire prevented the soldiers from moving forward. General Norman Cota approached the battalion and asked, "What outfit is this?" Someone yelled, "5th Rangers!" General Cota responded, "Well ... then, Rangers, lead the way!" The Rangers did lead the way. Since then, Rangers have used this phrase as their motto.

Fact

The RAAWS is often called the Goose after its inventor, Carl Gustav.

warhead—the part of a missile that carries explosives

TRANSPORTATION

Missions take Rangers into all kinds of environments. They might have to cross mountains, jungles, swamps, or deserts. On the ground, they use vehicles from motorbikes to jeeps.

Ranger Special Operations Vehicle (RSOV)

The Ranger Special Operations Vehicle (RSOV) was created specifically for the 75th Ranger Regiment. Each of the Ranger battalions has at least 12 RSOVs.

The RSOV is designed for a crew of three, but it can carry up to seven passengers.

The vehicle can be equipped with an MK19 grenade launcher and .50-caliber machine gun. It also usually carries at least one mounted 7.62 mm machine gun.

Motorcycles

Rangers use motorcycles to quickly move throughout an area. The Kawasaki L250D8 can be dropped on a pallet from a helicopter to Rangers below. The smaller Suzuki DS80 can be dropped with a parachute.

The RSOV is small enough to fit inside a Chinook helicopter or C-130 cargo plane, making them easy to transport.

Stryker Infantry Combat Vehicles

When in heavy combat, Rangers need a fully armored vehicle. They also need a protected vehicle when traveling through areas where mines or explosive devices might be in the way. The Stryker is a fully armored vehicle that Rangers rely on for many missions. The Stryker weighs about 19 tons (17 metric tons). It can travel more than 60 miles (97 km) per hour with a full squad of Rangers.

Each Ranger battalion also has medical RSOVs. Instead of weapons, these RSOVs have racks for carrying wounded soldiers.

OPERATION GOTHIC SERPENT
Somalia, 1993

BACKGROUND: In the early 1990s, Somalia was in a civil war and was experiencing food shortages. To help bring order to the country, U.S. special operations units conducted Operation Gothic Serpent.

RANGER MISSION: Capture enemy leaders who were in a building in Mogadishu.

an Apache helicopter flying over Mogadishu, Somalia, in 1993

Fact

The movie *Black Hawk Down* is based on the Rangers' battle in Mogadishu.

THE EVENTS:

Four teams of Rangers fast-roped from Black Hawk helicopters and set up positions around the building. Other special ops soldiers entered the building and captured the men they were looking for. However, Somali troops in nearby buildings began shooting at the Rangers.

soldiers who took part in the operations in Mogadishu

In the battle, an RPG hit a Black Hawk helicopter. The helicopter crashed, killing two pilots and injuring two crewmen. Some of the Rangers at the building fought their way to the crash site to help the injured soldiers.

With the Somali prisoners secured, the rest of the Rangers also tried to reach the crashed helicopter. But heavy gunfire and smoke made it impossible. The Rangers returned to their base with the prisoners.

The soldiers who had gone to the crash site to help were surrounded and trapped. Coming under very heavy fire, they moved into several buildings for shelter. For the next several hours, they fought nonstop to survive.

Somali soldiers attacked again and again. U.S. helicopters flew overhead, firing at enemy soldiers to keep them at a distance.

Rangers back at their base made a second attempt to reach the crash site. But the Somali militia controlled the streets. The Rangers had to turn back because they were outnumbered by enemy forces.

The trapped Rangers and special ops soldiers were under constant attack all night. They ran short of water and ammunition, but they kept fighting. Finally, after more than 10 hours of combat, relief arrived. One hundred ground vehicles fought their way to the crash site and rescued the soldiers.

Air Transport

When Rangers need to travel a long distance quickly, they take to the air.

The Chinook is the only U.S. Army helicopter that can land on water.

08-0

UNITED STATES ARM

Two RSOVs can fit inside.

C-130 HERCULES

This airplane carries large groups of Rangers. It also carries their RSOVs, motorcycles, and other ground vehicles. Upon arriving at a battle site, Rangers might parachute from the plane. If the mission is seizing an airport, the planes will land and deliver the Rangers' vehicles after the airfield is secure.

CH·47 CHINOOK HELICOPTER

This helicopter is used to move large numbers of soldiers or supplies. Side gun-ports can hold machine guns. It can fly with the rear ramp open, and a third machine gun can be placed there.

It can carry up to 44 special ops troops.

MH·6 Little Bird

AH·6 ATTACK AND MH·6 LITTLE BIRD HELICOPTERS

Nicknamed the "Killer Egg," the AH-6 helicopter can be fitted with guns, missiles, or rockets. Smaller than other helicopters, it can go into areas where larger helicopters cannot fly safely. The AH-6 provides air support to protect soldiers in combat on the ground.

The MH-6 Little Bird has benches for carrying up to six men. It is often used for quickly landing small groups of Rangers in combat areas and picking them up after their mission.

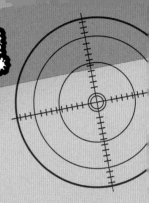

IN ACTION!

OPERATION JUST CAUSE
Panama, 1989

BACKGROUND AND RANGER MISSION: In 1989
the United States invaded Panama to remove dictator
Manuel Noriega from power. One of the missions given to
the 75th Ranger Regiment was to seize Rio Hato Airfield.

a C-130 Hercules flying over
the coast of Panama during
Operation Just Cause

dictator—a ruler who takes complete control of a country, often unjustly

1. On the night of December 20, 1989, Rangers parachuted onto the airfield from 13 C-130 Hercules airplanes. Panamanian Defense Forces (PDF) fired on the planes with small arms. Dodging enemy fire, the Rangers attacked the PDF barracks. They captured prisoners and cleared the airfield.

2. Rangers put up obstacles on the nearby road so enemy vehicles could not enter or leave the airfield. Once in control of the roads, Rangers secured buildings around the airfield.

3. U.S. aircraft landed, bringing in the Rangers' vehicles and motorcycles. Jeep and motorcycle teams moved out and set up positions away from the airport. By sunrise, Rangers had almost completely secured the airfield.

4. The Rangers' next task was to secure a nearby village and other buildings in the area. However, the Rangers faced intense enemy fire from a sniper in a building. Unable to move forward, they radioed for air support. Little Bird helicopters flew in. The helicopters fired on the building, removing the threat from the sniper. After the helicopter attack, the Rangers finished securing the buildings.

Rio Hato Airfield

ALWAYS READY

Rangers are a key element in the United States' war on **terrorism**. These highly-trained soldiers are heroic, intelligent, and creative as they carry out their missions. Using some of the most advanced weapons available, they surprise and overwhelm the enemy. Their battlefields are cities, mountains, jungles, swamps, and deserts.

As the nature of war changes, Rangers will change too. They will train to face new enemies. They will use technology to be even better equipped for combat. They will always be prepared to go anywhere in the world on a moment's notice. They will continue to fight for the United States and protect its people.

terrorism—use of violence and destructive acts to create fear and to achieve a political or religious goal

RANGERS LEAD THE WAY!

GLOSSARY

ally (AL-eye)—a person or country united with another for a common purpose

ambush (AM-bush)—a surprise attack

artillery (ar-TIL-uh-ree)—large guns, such as cannons or missile launchers, that require several soldiers to load, aim, and fire

barracks (BEAR-uhks)—housing for soldiers

bunker (BUHNG-kuhr)—a strongly built room or building set beneath the ground to offer protection during war

colonist (KAH-luh-nist)—a person who settles in a new territory governed by his or her home country

dictator (DIK-tay-tuhr)—a ruler who takes complete control of a country, often unjustly

navigation (NAV-uh-gay-shun)—the science of plotting and following a course from one place to another

raid (RAYD)—a sudden, surprise attack on a place

reconnaissance (ree-KAH-nuh-suhnss)—a mission to gather information about an enemy

tactic (TAK-tik)—an action taken to achieve a goal

terrorism (TER-ur-i-zuhm)—use of violence and destructive acts to create fear and to achieve a political or religious goal

warhead (WOR-hed)—the part of a missile that carries explosives

READ MORE

Cooke, Tim. *U.S.* Army Rangers. Ultimate Special Forces. New York: PowerKids Press, 2013.

Harasymiw, Mark A. *Rangers.* U.S. Special Forces. New York: Gareth Stevens Pub., 2012.

Vanderhoof, Gabrielle and C. F. Earl. Army Rangers. Special Forces: Protecting, Building, Teaching, and Fighting. Broomall, Penn.: Mason Crest Pub., 2011.

INTERNET SITES

FactHound offers a safe, fun way to find Internet sites related to this book. All of the sites on FactHound have been researched by our staff.

Here's all you do:

Visit www.facthound.com

Type in this code: 9781429686594

INDEX